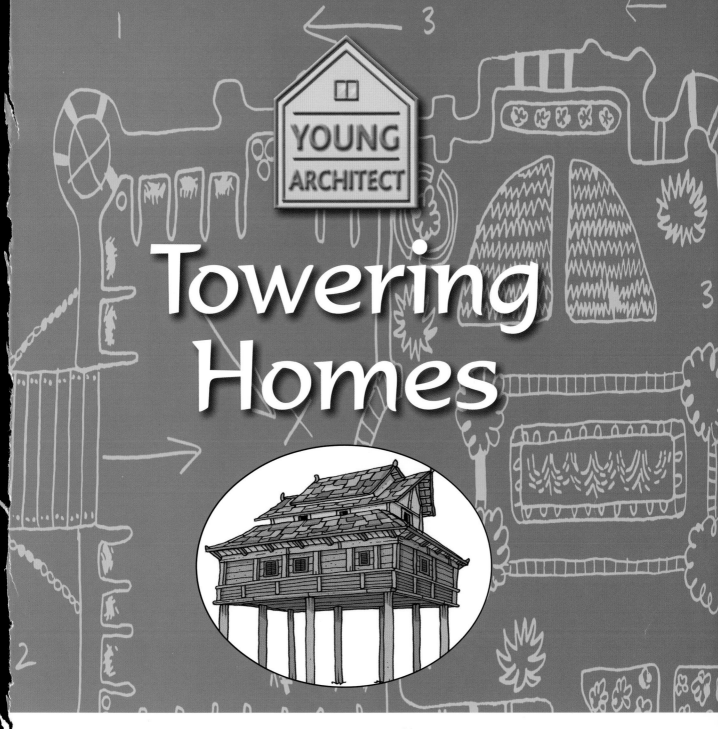

YOUNG ARCHITECT

Towering Homes

by Gerry Bailey

Illustrated by Moreno Chiacchiera, Michelle Todd, and Joelle Dreidemy

Crabtree Publishing Company

Crabtree Publishing Company
www.crabtreebooks.com
1-800-387-7650

Published in Canada
616 Welland Ave.
St. Catharines, ON
L2M 5V6

Published in the United States
PMB 59051, 350 Fifth Ave.
59th Floor,
New York, NY

Author: Gerry Bailey
Illustrators: Moreno Chiacchiera, Michelle Todd,
   Joelle Dreidemy
Project coordinator: Kelly McNiven
Editor: Kathy Middleton
Proofreader: Crystal Sikkens
Print and Production coordinator and
   Prepress technician: Margaret Amy Salter

Photographs:
Pg 4   DyMax
Pg 10   Goran Bogicevic / Shutterstock.com
Pg 11   (tl) ldambles; (tr) Francois Etienne;
        du Plessis; (bl)Alaettin YILDIRIM
Pg 13   Radakaren
Pg 14/15   Dan Kaplan
Pg 16/17   Stock Connection / SuperStock
Pg 18   (t) Meiqianbao; (b) Rufous
Pg 19   jejim
Pg 20   stable
Pg 22   Robert Huberman / SuperStock
Pg 25   Fedor Selivanov
Pg 28   pistolseven

All images are Shutterstock.com unless otherwise stated.

Every attempt has been made to clear copyright. Should there be any
inadvertent omission, please apply to the publisher for rectification.

Printed in Hong Kong/092013/BK20130703

Library and Archives Canada Cataloguing in Publication

Bailey, Gerry, author
    Towering homes / by Gerry Bailey ; illustrated by Moreno Chiacchiera,
Michelle Todd and Joelle Dreidemy.

(Young architect)
Includes index.
Issued in print and electronic formats.
ISBN 978-0-7787-0289-4 (bound).--ISBN 978-0-7787-0299-3 (pbk.).--
ISBN 978-1-4271-1278-1 (pdf).--ISBN 978-1-4271-1274-3 (html)

    1. Tall buildings--Juvenile literature. 2. Architecture, Domestic--Juvenile
literature. I. Chiacchiera, Moreno, illustrator II. Todd, Michelle, 1978-,
illustrator III. Dreidemy, Joelle, illustrator IV. Title.

NA6230.B33 2013   j728   C2013-904071-4
                                        C2013-904072-2

Library of Congress Cataloging-in-Publication Data

Bailey, Gerry.
 Towering homes / Written by Gerry Bailey ; Illustrated by Moreno Chiacchiera,
Michelle Todd, and Joelle Dreidemy.
    pages cm. -- (Young architect)
 Includes index.
 ISBN 978-0-7787-0289-4 (reinforced library binding) -- ISBN 978-0-7787-0299-3 (pbk.) --
ISBN 978-1-4271-1278-1 (electronic pdf) -- ISBN 978-1-4271-1274-3 (electronic html)
 1. Tall buildings--Juvenile literature. 2. Architecture, Domestic--Juvenile literature. I.
Chiacchiera, Moreno, illustrator. II. Title.

  NA6230.B33 2013
  728--dc23

                     2013023899

Contents

4–5	A pile of homes	18–19	Rising to a point
6–7	Stories	20–21	Raising the bridge
8–9	Architect's words:	22–23	Perched on the rocks
	Elevator; Escalator;	24	On a tilt
	Stairs; Fire escape	25	Architect's tools:
10–11	Glass and steel		Plumb line
12	Architect's words:	26–27	Raised on stilts
	Foundations	28–29	Stilts in water
13	Architect's tools:	30	Glossary
	Scale model	31	Learning more
14–15	Layer on top of layer	32	Index
16–17	Cave homes		

Introduction

Some people like to live in a house that is close to the ground, such as a small cottage or a single-**story** home. But many people enjoy living high above the ground. Today, apartment buildings and office skyscrapers are built tall so they can hold hundreds of people. Many buildings look like giant needles pointing up toward the sky. Others are pyramid-shaped towers. Some sit high up on stilts so they are protected from water or dangerous animals.

Do you dream of becoming an architect? Read about the many kinds of buildings that tower above the ground—buildings you may design yourself one day!

A pile of homes

As more and more people move into towns and cities, there is often not enough land to build homes for all of them. The city has to grow upward instead of outward.

Tall buildings take up less room and can hold a lot of people. Although these homes, called apartments, are stacked on top of each other, there are many parts of the building that people can share.

There may be a **basement** with a garage for everyone's cars, a laundry room for everyone to use, shared garbage areas, playgrounds, stores—and sometimes even a swimming pool.

This tall building is home to hundreds of people.

Stories

An apartment building is made up of a lot of floors, called stories, stacked on top of each other.

The main entrance is at ground level.

On the ground floor, there may be stores and restaurants.

Stories are connected by staircases and at least one elevator.

Each apartment has a living room, kitchen, bedrooms, and a bathroom.

At the top of the building are very large apartments called penthouses. They often have a great view of the city!

A basement room is used for laundry.

In really expensive apartment buildings, the roof can be used as a place where helicopters can land!

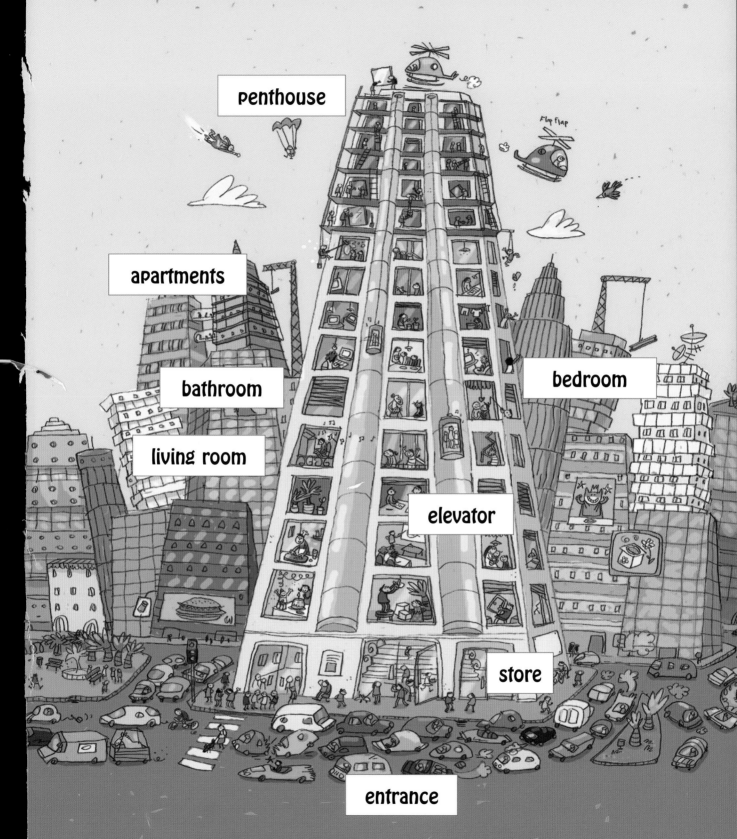

penthouse

apartments

bathroom

living room

bedroom

elevator

store

entrance

- Architect's words -

ELEVATOR: An elevator is used to carry people or goods to the many floors of tall buildings. It is like a box that is hauled up and down by a system of pulleys. An elevator's doors open when it reaches the level of the floor it is stopping at. The pulley cables have to be strong and long-lasting because elevators are in constant use.

ESCALATOR: An **escalator** is a moving staircase. Its steps are pulled by a chain that moves in circles which is powered by a motor.

STAIRS: Stairs are steps that people climb inside or outside a building. They are built on a frame or staircase, and have a railing to hold onto. The stairs are one of the strongest parts of a building.

FIRE ESCAPE: A fire is a very dangerous situation in a tall building, since elevators and stairs cannot be used to escape. In order to get out, people can use a **fire escape** instead. A fire escape is a series of iron platforms connected by steps. They are located on the outside walls of the building.

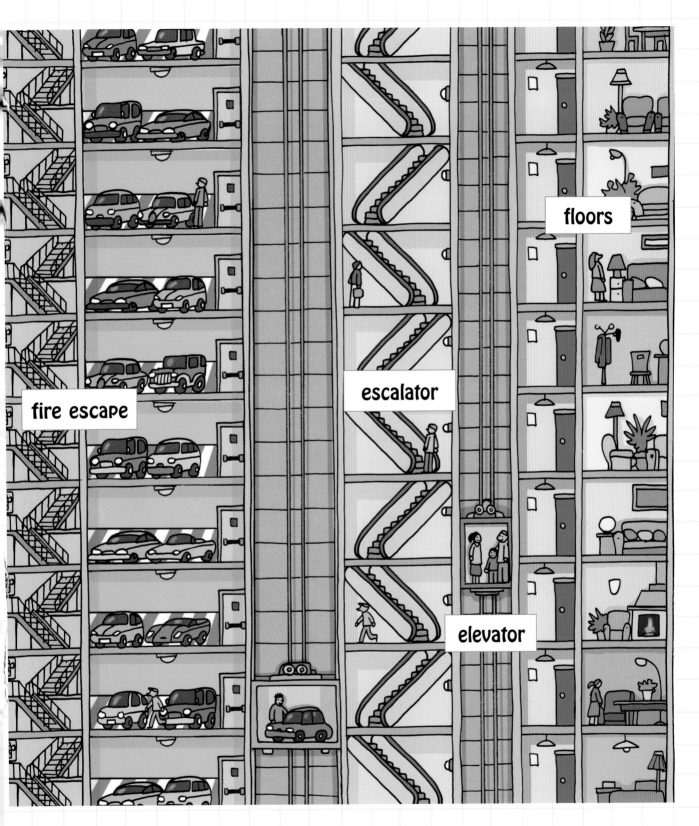

fire escape

escalator

floors

elevator

Glass and steel

Three main materials are used to build apartment buildings and office skyscrapers. These are **glass**, reinforced **concrete**, and **steel**. A frame of steel girders, or **beams**, carries the weight of the building's whole structure.

The Burj Khalifa in Dubai has 28,000 glass panels. It stands 2,625 feet (800 meters) tall.

GLASS: Glass is made by heating a special sand until it is a liquid, and then cooling it.

CONCRETE: Concrete is a mix of water, cement powder, and gravel or sand. It is poured around steel rods called rebars. The rebars strengthen the concrete when it dries, making it less likely to crack or break in a strong wind.

STEEL: Steel is a mix of iron and carbon. These are melted at very high temperatures and poured into molds to cool and become solid.

- Architect's words -

FOUNDATIONS:

It is important that a very tall building does not lean or fall over. To prevent this from happening, the frame of the building goes deep into the ground. Huge blocks or cylinders of concrete, called piles, are sunk into the hard rock that lies below the soil on top of the ground. These piles are called the foundation. Some skyscrapers use nearly 200 piles in their foundation. For very high skyscrapers, these piles may reach as far down as 164 feet (50 meters).

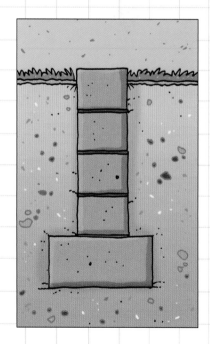

Shallow foundations made of concrete will support only a low structure.

Piles are driven deep into the ground by a heavy weight. Deep piles will support a tall structure.

12

piles

foundation

- Architect's tools -

SCALE MODEL:

Architects often make a scale model of a building before it is built. A scale model is an exact copy of the actual building shrunk down and used a guide.

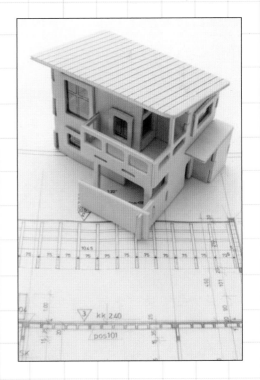

Layer on top of layer

A Native American people, called the Pueblo people by Spanish explorers, lived in villages in the southwest of the United States. The land is made up of steep canyons and deserts.

The Pueblo people were named after the multi-family houses they built. *Pueblo* is the Spanish word for village. Their houses were made of adobe—a mixture of sand, clay, water, and dried grasses such as straw. These materials were mixed, baked into hard **bricks**, and used to build Pueblo homes.

The Pueblo people built their homes one on top of the other, like multi-story apartment buildings. The higher apartments were reached by climbing a ladder. The Pueblo people were experts at making pottery. They also raised turkeys and grew corn, pumpkins, and beans.

Some Pueblo homes are still in use.

15

Cave homes

Imagine living in a cave! In the province of Shaanxi, in China, this would not seem so extraordinary. About 40 million people in Shaanxi still live in cave homes just like their ancestors did hundreds of years ago.

Most of the cave homes are built into the side of a cliff. The soft yellow earth found in the region is easy to scrape out. Each **arched** entrance leads into a long room inside. The caves stay cool in summer and warm and cozy in winter. Most caves have modern plumbing, electricity, and telephone service.

A large community lives in these caves in Shaanxi province, China.

Rising to a point

The twin pagodas of Taiyuan City, China, tower 180 feet (55 meters) high.

Pagodas are tall buildings built in **tiers** that rise to a point at the top. Building in tiers not only makes a structure more stable, it also makes it look very beautiful.

Pagodas were first built in China, then spread to most of Southeast Asia. Buddhist monks stored sacred writings and **relics** in pagodas.

A Chinese temple

Traditionally, pagodas are built with an odd number of levels for good luck. They are often decorated with carvings. Many show the Buddha, a religious leader. But some also have animal carvings of birds, lions, monkeys, and mythical beasts such as dragons.

A pagoda can be built into the side of a cliff. This is Shibaozhai Pagoda in Shibao, Chongqing, China.

19

Raising the bridge

Castles were not just homes, they were **fortifications** built to protect the people who lived in them. They were often built on hilltops to make them even harder to attack.

The keep was the main tower. It was usually made of wood or stone and built on a human-made hill called a **motte**. A ditch, or moat, was dug around the castle and filled with water. The only access to the castle was across a bridge that could be lowered or raised. It was known as a drawbridge.

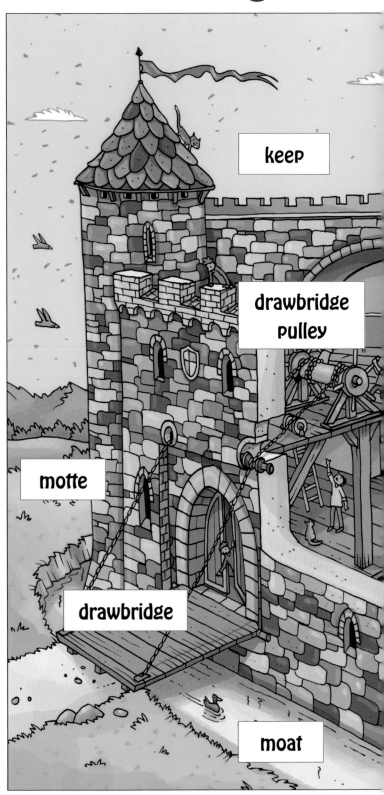

keep

drawbridge pulley

motte

drawbridge

moat

A SIMPLE SYSTEM

A drawbridge is a simple mechanism that uses a system of cords or cables and pulleys to raise the bridge. More complicated pulley systems also use a turning screw called a winch. When the winch is turned, the cables tighten and raise the bridge.

The cables pass through pulleys.

The cables are pulled to lift the bridge.

A modern drawbridge such as Tower Bridge in London, England, uses oil-powered machinery to lift the bridge in two parts in the middle.

This drawbridge leads to the entrance of the keep.

Perched on the rocks

Taktsang Monastery in Bhutan

The Taktsang Monastery in the Himalayan kingdom of Bhutan is also known as the "Tiger's Nest." It got its name from a legend that is hundreds of years old. It was said that a wise man named Guru Rinpoche flew on the back of a female tiger to a cave above the Paro Valley. He meditated, or sat thinking, in the cave for many months. It became a holy place for Buddhist monks to visit.

In 1692, the Taktsang Monastery was built close to the holy cave. It is a spectacular building.

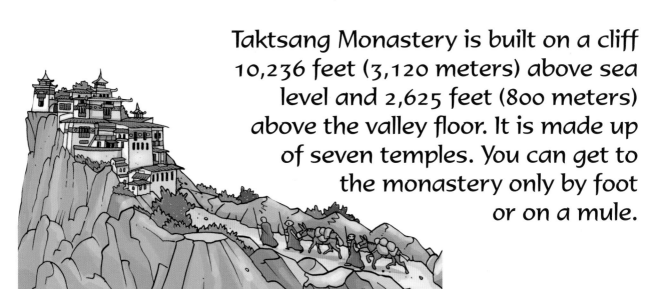

Taktsang Monastery is built on a cliff 10,236 feet (3,120 meters) above sea level and 2,625 feet (800 meters) above the valley floor. It is made up of seven temples. You can get to the monastery only by foot or on a mule.

On a tilt

It looks as if it's about to topple over. But the Leaning Tower of Pisa, in Italy, still stands after more than 800 years. It was supposed to be upright but started to lean during construction. It is actually a bell tower, or **campanile**, with the bell chamber on the eighth and highest story.

The Tower of Pisa is 197 feet (60 meters) tall and, until 1990 it leaned at an angle of 5.5 degrees. Various attempts were made to prevent the tower from leaning more or even falling over. Then, starting in the 1990s, wedges of earth were slowly removed from below the north side of the tower over a period of nearly ten years.

Slowly, the foundation began to sink back into the gap that had been left. This brought the tower back to an angle that was a little safer.

Architect's tools

- Plumb line -

A **plumb line** is a heavy weight, often made of lead, that hangs from a string. It is used by builders to check that the walls of a building are vertical. This means the walls rise at a 90-degree angle to the ground.

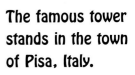

The famous tower stands in the town of Pisa, Italy.

25

thatch

bamboo matting

beams

studs

cement

stilts

decking boards

26

Raised on stilts

How do you protect your home from wild animals or from flooding? You build it on top of columns called stilts. Stilt houses exist in many parts of the world. Some are so high, you might wonder how they stay up!

Markers on the ground show where each corner of the house will be.

Stilts are driven into the ground, one at each corner and one in between the corners. They are sunk into cement.

Boards are attached to the stilts in rows. Then decking boards are laid across these to make the floor.

Vertical boards, called studs, and horizontal boards, called beams and joists, frame the walls, ceiling, and roof. Tiles or thatch are placed over the frame of the roof.

Wall materials, such as bamboo matting, are attached to the wall boards leaving open spaces for doors and windows.

Some kelongs are built on their own. Others are built in tiny villages. Wooden gangways, or bridges, connect them to the land.

28

Stilts in water

Homes built over the water usually stand on stilts. The stilts keep them high above water levels even in floods.

A **kelong** is a stilt building found in Southeast Asia. Smaller ones were built originally as platforms to fish from, but larger kelongs are used as homes.

A kelong is built without using nails. The wooden planks and tree trunks from which it is made are bound together with rattan instead. Rattan is the stem of a thin, flexible palm. The wooden stilts on which the houses sit are around 65 feet (20 meters) long. They sink about 20 feet (6 meters) into the seabed.

planks

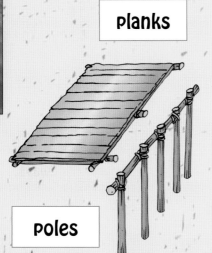

Planks and poles are bound together to make docks for boats and walkways between the houses.

poles

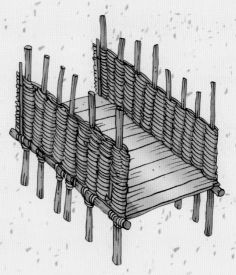

29

Glossary

arched Curved at the top

basement The room in the bottom of a building, often below ground level

beam A strong piece of wood used to support parts of a building

brick A rectangular block made of a mixture of clay and other materials that has been hardened by heating

campanile Another name for a bell tower

concrete A mixture of cement, sand, and other rocks that sets to a hard material

elevator A compartment or platform in a vertical shaft that carries people or goods up or down in a building

escalator A mechanical staircase

fire escape A staircase, often on an outside wall, that leads from top stories to the ground

fortification Something that strengthens or defends

glass A tough material you can see through made from a mix of heated sand and other materials

kelong A type of house in Southeast Asia that is built on stilts

motte A raised mound on which a castle is built

plumb line A tool used to measure the straight edge of a wall

relic An object that is kept in remembrance of a person, place, or event

steel A strong metal made of a mix of iron and other elements, used in building

story Another name for a floor or level of a building

tiers Layers or rows arranged one above another

Learning more

Books:

Earth-Friendly Buildings, Bridges and More.
Etta Karner. Kids Can Press, 2012.
Information on green engineering and simple
activities provide an eco-friendly resource
for budding engineers and architects.

*Look At That Building! A First Book of
Structures.* Scot Ritchie. Kids Can
Press, 2011.
Five friends set out to build a doghouse
and explore basic construction concepts
including foundations, frames, and other
building fundamentals.

The Tallest Buildings. Susan K. Mitchell.
Gareth Stevens, 2008.
This book explores some of the tallest,
longest, and biggest structures found
around the world.

Websites:

PBS's Building Big video and website:
www.pbs.org/wgbh/buildingbig/
This website includes activities as it explores
bridges, skyscrapers, and more.

Archkidecture:
www.archkidecture.org/
This website gives a lot of basic information
on architecture for kids.

The Great Buildings Collection:
www.greatbuildings.com/
Readers receive design and architectural
information on a thousand buildings
from around the world.

Structures Around the World: Activities for
the Elementary Classroom:
www.exploratorium.edu/structures/
Readers learn all about structures through
hands-on activities provided by the
Exploratorium museum.

Try Engineering:
www.tryengineering.org/lesson.php
This website features lessons plans and
activities that explore engineering principles.

Index

adobe 14

apartment 3, 5, 6, 7, 15

bamboo 26

basement 5, 6

bathroom 6, 7

beam 26, 27

bedroom 6, 7

bell tower 24

board 27

brick 14

cable 8, 21

campanile 24

carbon 11

carving 18

castle 20

cave 17, 23

cement 11, 26, 27

clay 14

concrete 10, 11, 12

decking 26, 27

drawbridge 20, 21

electricity 17

elevator 6, 7, 8

entrance 6, 7, 17, 21

escalator 8

fire escape 8

fortification 20

foundation 12, 13, 24

frame 8, 10

gangway 28

girder 10

glass 10, 11

gravel 11

helicopter 6, 7

iron 11

joist 27

keep 20, 21

kelong 28, 29

kitchen 6

ladder 15

living room 6, 7

moat 20

motor 8

motte 20

pagoda 18, 19

palm 29

penthouse 6, 7

pile 12, 13

plank 29

platform 8, 29

playground 5

plumbing 17

plumb line 25

pole 29

Pueblo 14, 15

pulley 8, 20, 21

rail 8

rattan 29

rock 12

sand 11, 14

scale model 13

skyscraper 3, 6, 10, 12

staircase 6, 8

steel 10, 11

stilts/stilt house 3, 26, 27, 29

store 5, 6, 7

story 3, 6, 24

straw 14

stud 27

Taktsang Monastery 22, 23

telephone 17

temple 18, 23

thatch 26, 27

tile 27

Tower Bridge 21

Tower of Pisa 24, 25

walkway 29

wall 8, 25, 27

winch 21